Read for a Better World™

SPINOSAURUS
A First Look

JERI RANCH

GRL Consultant, Diane Craig, Certified Literacy Specialist

Lerner Publications ◆ Minneapolis

Educator Toolbox

Reading books is a great way for kids to express what they're interested in. Before reading this title, ask the reader these questions:

What do you think this book is about? Look at the cover for clues.

What do you already know about this dinosaur?

What do you want to learn about this dinosaur?

Let's Read Together

Encourage the reader to use the pictures to understand the text.

Point out when the reader successfully sounds out a word.

Praise the reader for recognizing sight words such as *had* and *it*.

TABLE OF CONTENTS

Spinosaurus 4

You Connect! 21
STEM Snapshot 22
Photo Glossary 23
Learn More 23
Index 24

Spinosaurus

Spinosaurus is a kind of dinosaur. It lived 90 million years ago.

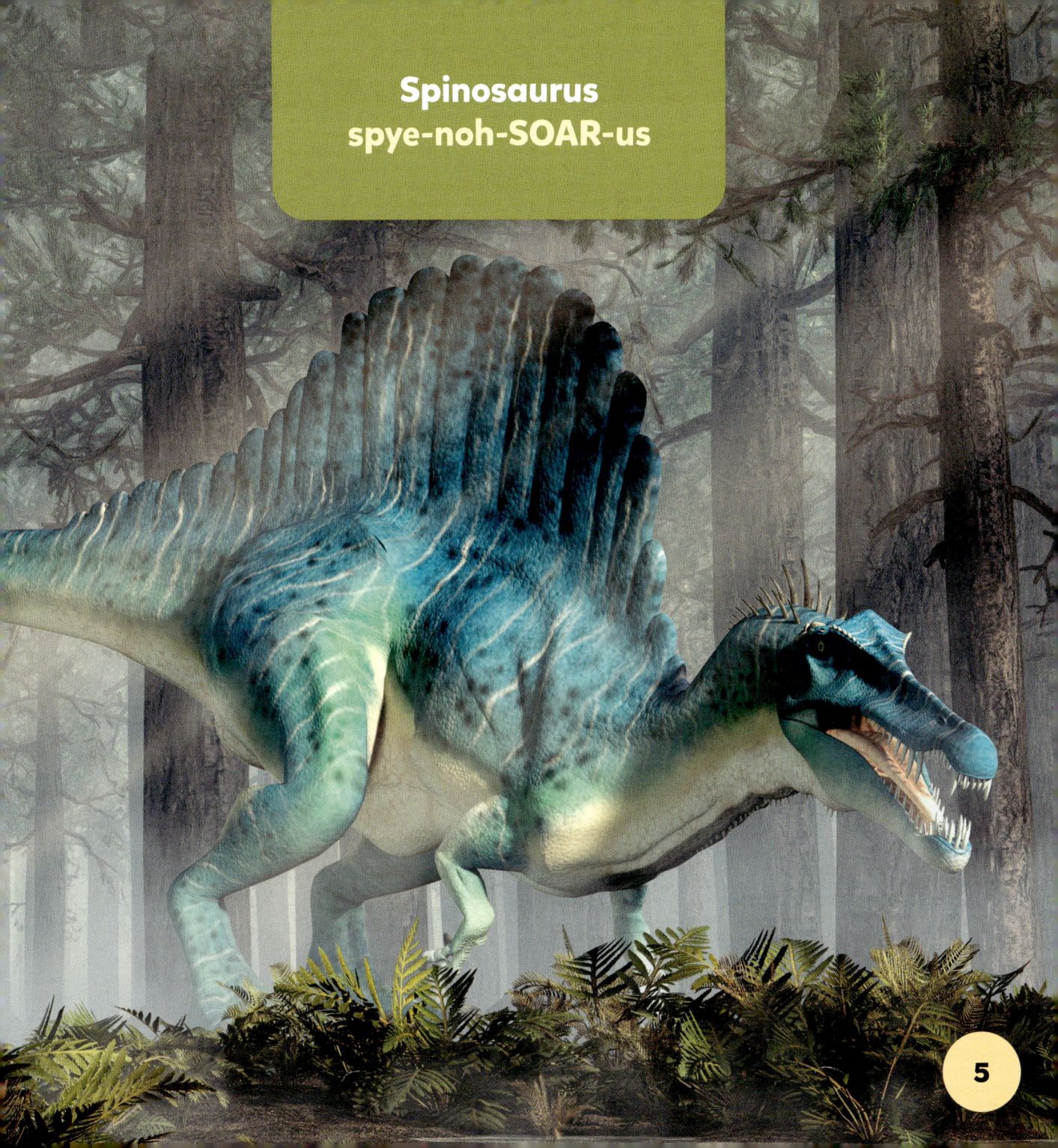

Spinosaurus
spye-noh-SOAR-us

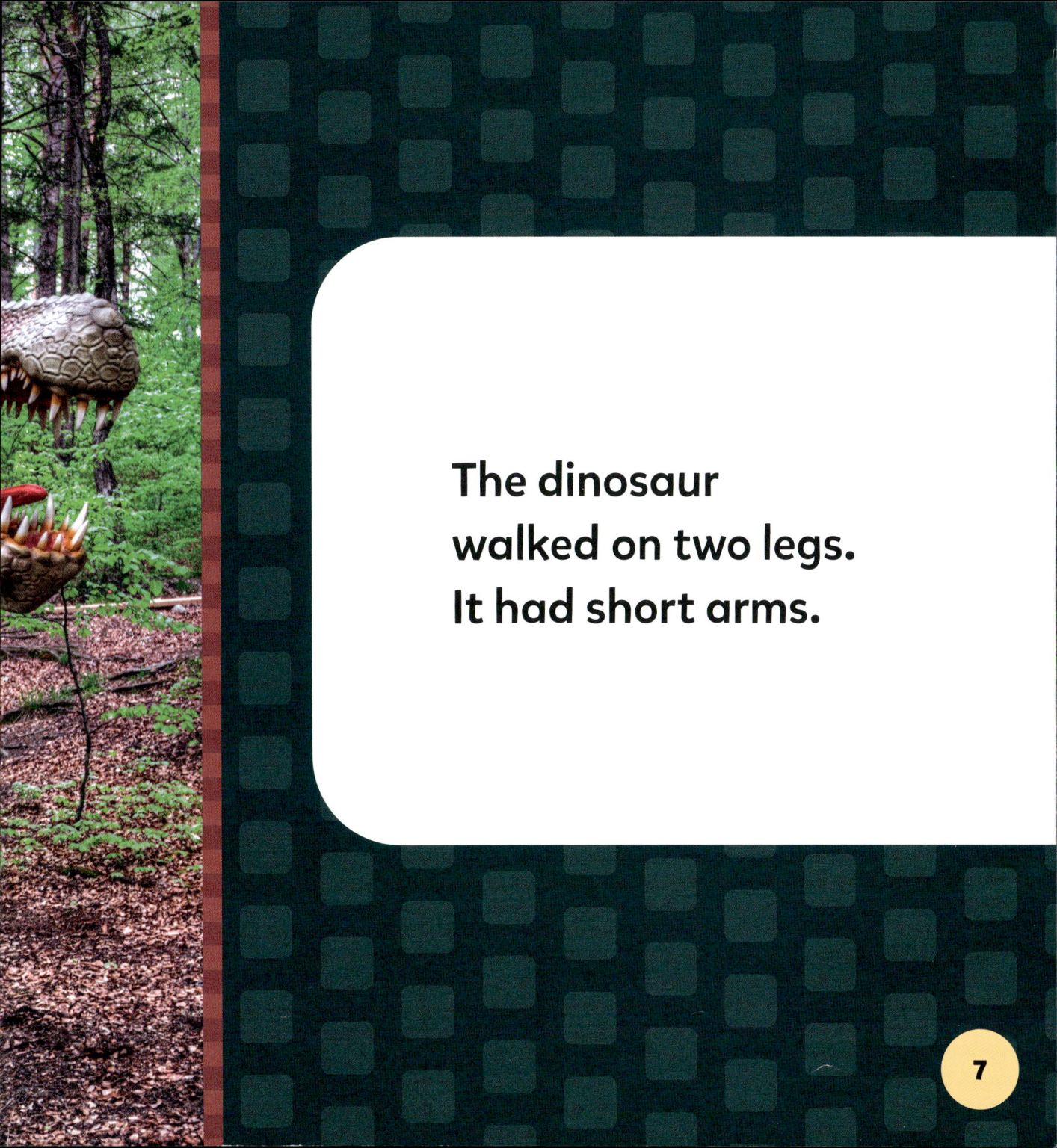

The dinosaur walked on two legs. It had short arms.

8

It was about as long as a humpback whale.

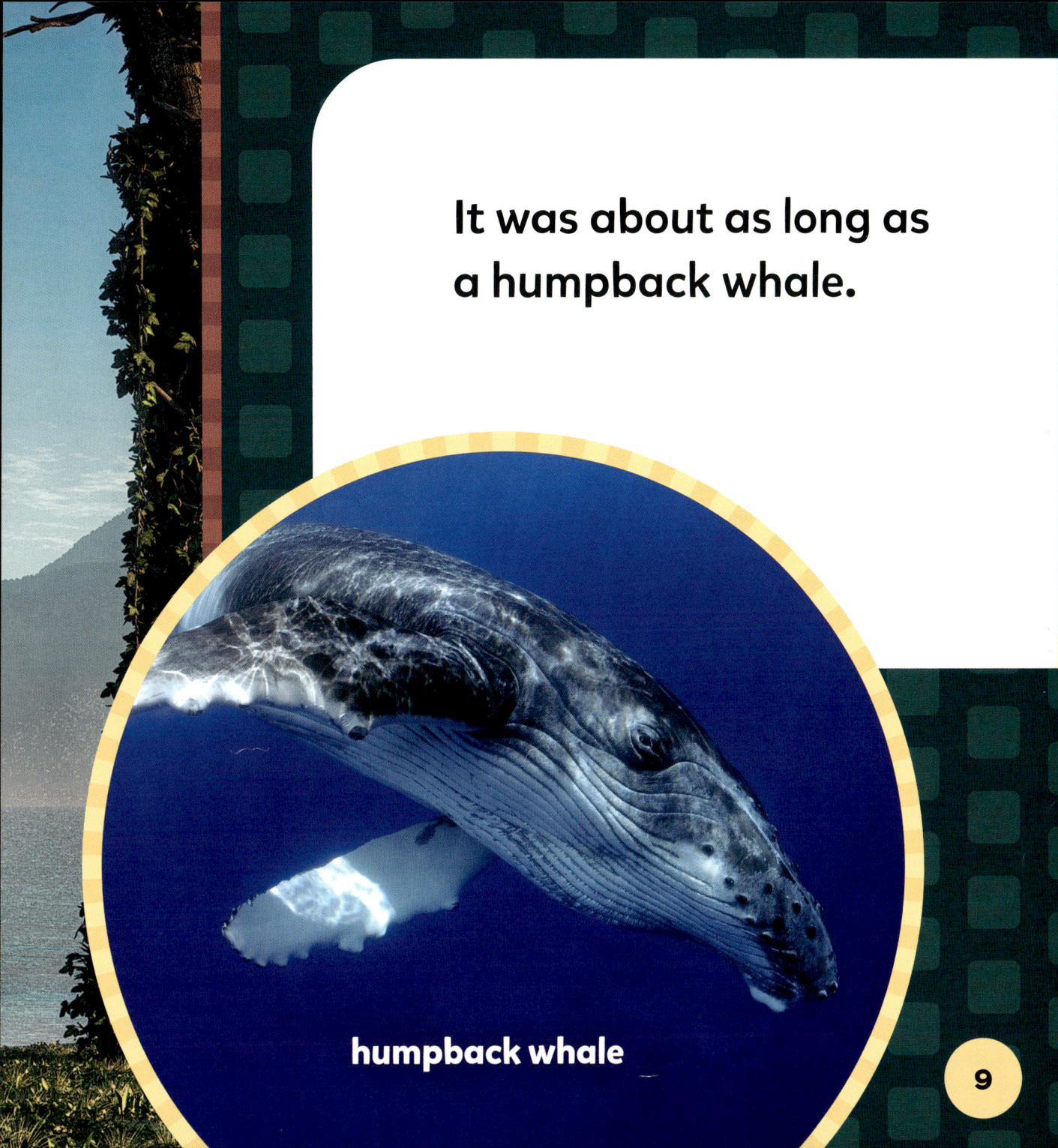

humpback whale

It had spines on its back.
They made a sail shape.

10

It lived near water. It may have been a good swimmer.

What other animals can swim?

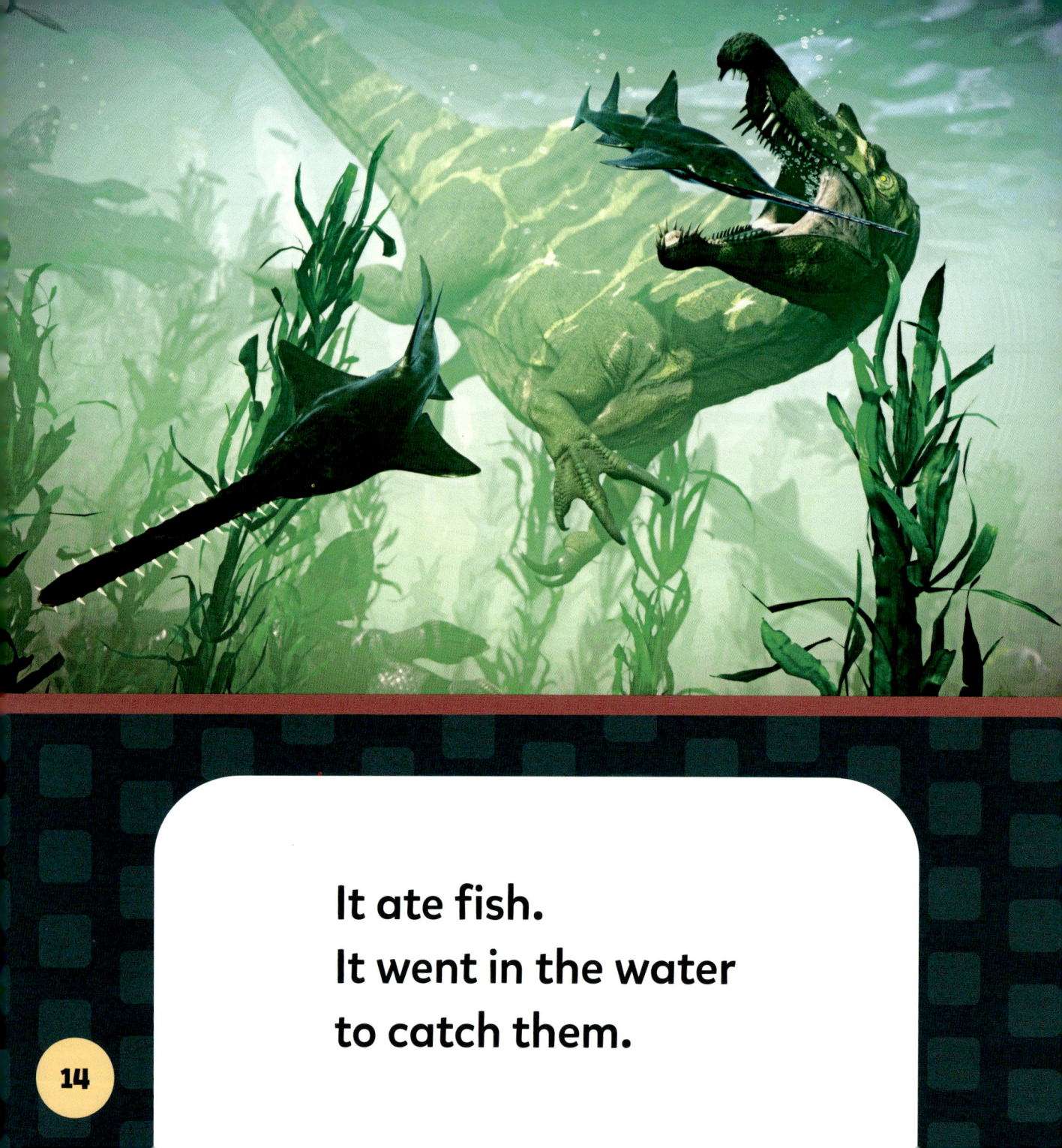

It ate fish.
It went in the water to catch them.

It ate land animals too.

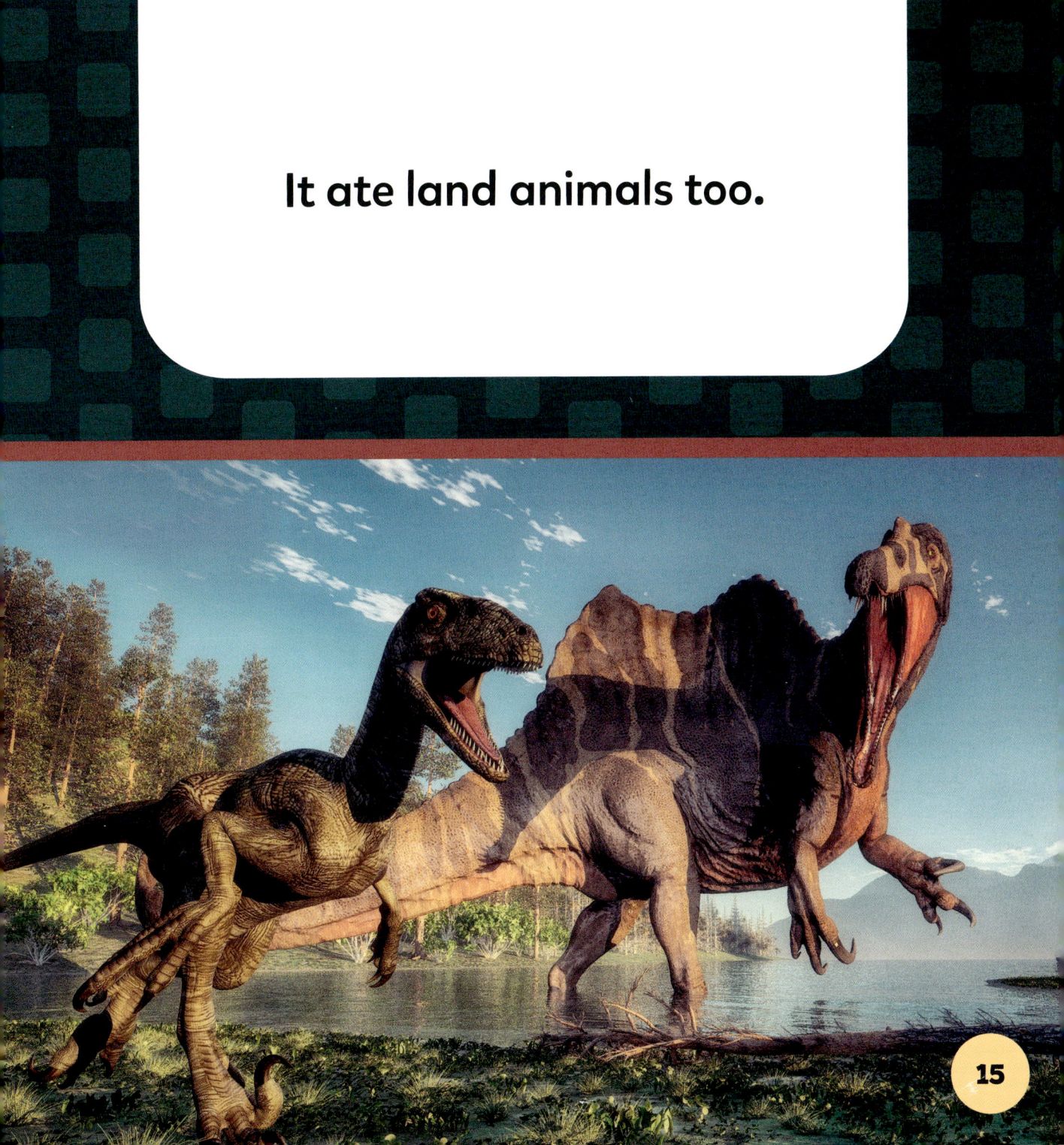

It had a long jaw. Its teeth were sharp.

How are sharp teeth useful?

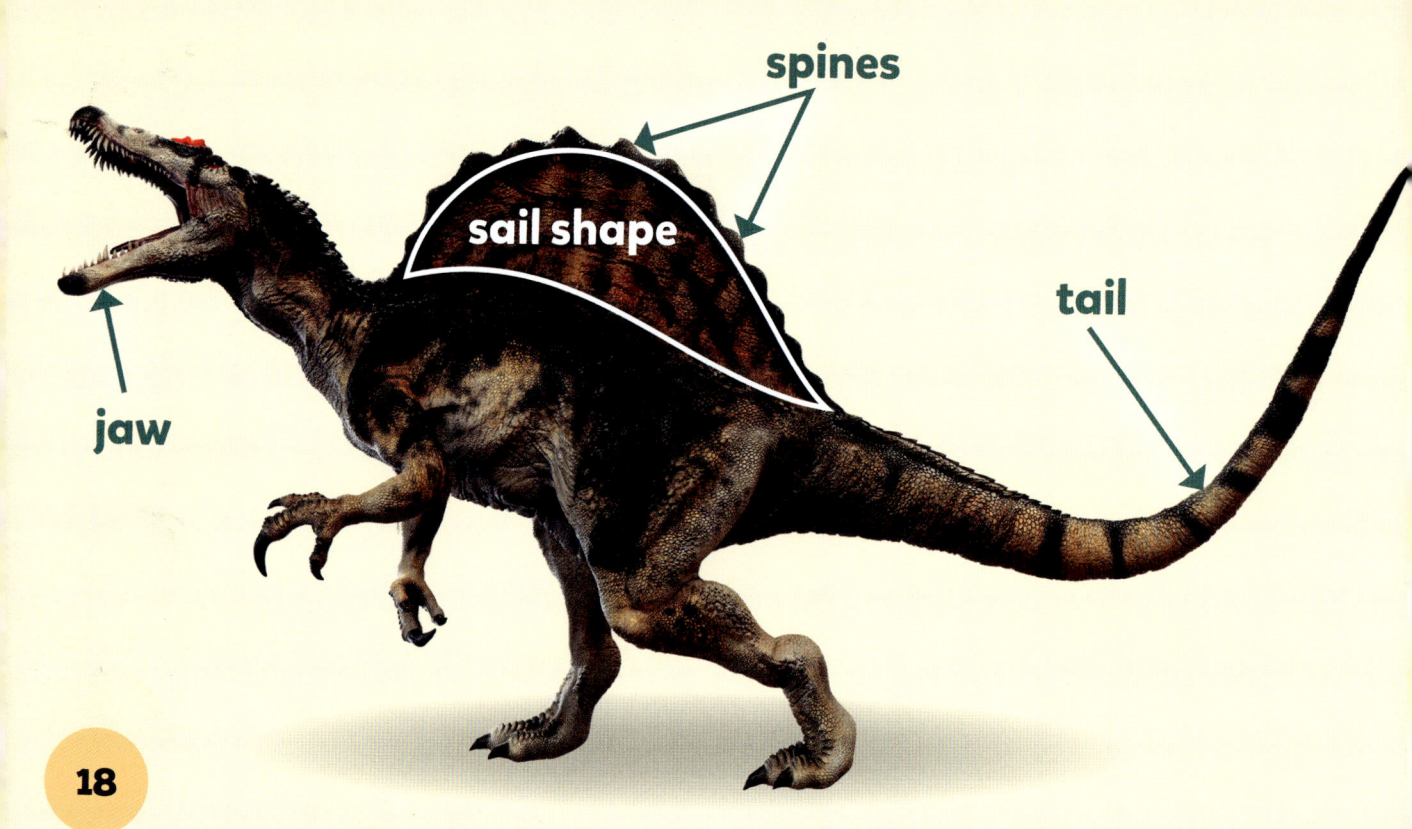

It had a long tail.

spines

sail shape

tail

jaw

18

How do tails help animals swim?

It may have been used to swim.

19

The dinosaur's bones help us learn more.

You Connect!

What is something you like about this dinosaur?

What else looks like this dinosaur?

What other dinosaurs do you know about?

STEM Snapshot

Encourage students to think and ask questions like scientists. Ask the reader:

What is something you learned about this dinosaur?

What is something you noticed in the pictures of the dinosaur?

What is something you still don't know about this dinosaur?

Photo Glossary

Learn More

Carr, Aaron. *Spinosaurus*. New York: AV2, 2022.

Nelson, Jake. *I'm a Spinosaurus*. Ann Arbor, MI: Cherry Lake Publishing, 2021.

Sabelko, Rebecca. *Spinosaurus*. Minneapolis: Bellwether Media, 2021.

Index

arms, 7
bones, 20
legs, 7
spines, 10
tail, 18, 19
teeth, 16, 17
water, 12, 14

Photo Acknowledgments

The images in this book are used with the permission of: © Daniel Eskridge/Shutterstock Images, pp. 4–5, 10–11, 16–17, 23 (jaw, spines); © bogonet/iStockphoto, pp. 6–7; © Orla/Shutterstock Images, pp. 8–9, 15; © Yann hubert/Shutterstock Images, pp. 9, 23 (humpback whale); © Orla/iStockphoto, p. 12; © Elenarts/Shutterstock Images, pp. 12–13; © Herschel Hoffmeyer/Shutterstock Images, pp. 14, 18, 19, 23 (fish); © Mike Bowler/Wikimedia Commons, p. 20.

Cover Photograph: © Daniel Eskridge/Shutterstock Images

Design Elements: © Mighty Media, Inc.

Copyright © 2024 by Lerner Publishing Group, Inc.

All rights reserved. International copyright secured. No part of this book may be reproduced, stored in a retrieval system, or transmitted in any form or by any means—electronic, mechanical, photocopying, recording, or otherwise—without the prior written permission of Lerner Publishing Group, Inc., except for the inclusion of brief quotations in an acknowledged review.

Lerner Publications Company
An imprint of Lerner Publishing Group, Inc.
241 First Avenue North
Minneapolis, MN 55401 USA

For reading levels and more information, look up this title at www.lernerbooks.com.

Main body text set in Mikado a Medium.
Typeface provided by Hannes von Doehren.

Library of Congress Cataloging-in-Publication Data

Names: Ranch, Jeri, author.
Title: Spinosaurus : a first look / by Jeri Ranch.
Description: Minneapolis : Lerner Publications , [2024] | Series: Read about dinosaurs (Read for a better world) | Includes bibliographical references and index. | Audience: Ages 5–8 | Audience: Grades K–1 | Summary: "A dinosaur the size of a humpback whale with spines on its back? Readers will be excited to learn about the Spinosaurus with leveled text and full-color images to help bring it to life"— Provided by publisher.
Identifiers: LCCN 2022039314 (print) | LCCN 2022039315 (ebook) | ISBN 9781728491349 (library binding) | ISBN 9798765603499 (paperback) | ISBN 9781728499307 (ebook)
Classification: LCC QE862.S3 R35868 2024 (print) | LCC QE862.S3 (ebook) | DDC 567.912–dc23/eng/20220824

LC record available at https://lccn.loc.gov/2022039314
LC ebook record available at https://lccn.loc.gov/2022039315

Manufactured in the United States of America
1 – CG – 7/15/23